Holiday Magic Books

Halloween
MAGIC

by James W. Baker
pictures by George Overlie

Lerner Publications Company ⌐ Minneapolis

To my son, James, who tricked me into my first public performance of magic one Halloween many years ago. He told his second grade teacher that his father was a magician who would be happy to come to the school and treat his classmates to a magic show.

This book is available in two editions:
Library binding by Lerner Publications Company
Soft cover by First Avenue Editions
241 First Avenue North
Minneapolis, Minnesota 55401

Library of Congress Cataloging-in-Publication Data

Baker, James W., 1926-
  Halloween magic/by James W. Baker; pictures by George Overlie.
    p.   cm.—(The Holiday magic books)
  Summary: Directions for ten magic tricks with a Halloween theme.
  ISBN 0-8225-2228-4 (lib. bdg.)
  ISBN 0-8225-9551-6 (pbk.)
  1. Tricks—Juvenile literature. 2. Halloween—Juvenile literature.
[1. Magic tricks. 2. Halloween.] I. Overlie, George, ill. II. Title.
III. Series: Baker, James W., 1926-   Holiday magic books.
GV1548.B334   1988   88-2718
793.8—dc19   CIP
                                                                        AC

Manufactured in the United States of America

  2 3 4 5 6 7 8 9 10 97 96 95 94 93 92 91 90 89

CONTENTS

INTRODUCTION

It is a dark and scary night. The wind howls through bare trees and bats swoop through the air. It is Halloween, the night when ghosts are about. You may be one of those ghosts, or you may be disguised as another creature. Whatever your costume, you have probably changed into a different being for the night.

Some children gather together at a friend's "haunted house" to bob for apples and scare each other at a Halloween party. Others trick-or-treat, going from house to house in search of candy and cookies. According to tradition, if they are not given a treat, they will play a trick on the people in that house.

Instead of playing tricks on other people, you may want to perform tricks. Learn to perform the magical illusions in this book, and you can bewitch your audience with Halloween magic.

GHOSTS ON THE ROOF

HOW IT LOOKS

You use a deck of playing cards to show how four ghosts went to haunt a house at Halloween. Using the four tens as ghosts, you place them in the house (the deck of cards) at different places. When you—the magician—come along, all four ghosts flee to the roof of the building. You show that the four tens are now on top of the pack of cards.

HOW TO MAKE IT

For this trick, you will need a deck of playing cards.

HOW TO DO IT

1. Before you start, place any three cards behind the four tens. Fan out the four tens in your hand, showing them to the audience and keeping the three extra cards hidden behind them (**Figure 1**). Explain that the tens are four ghosts on Halloween night and that the deck of cards is the house the four ghosts are planning to haunt.

Any three cards hidden behind the four tens

figure 1.

2. Close up the fan of four tens (along with the three cards hidden behind them) and place all seven cards on top of the deck, face down (**Figure 2**).

figure 2.

the four tens

Three extra cards

3. Explain that the first ghost entered the house through a window in the basement. Take the top card from the deck (supposedly a ten) and push it into the deck near the bottom. Don't let anyone see its face.

4. Saying that the second ghost went into the house by the front door, take the card on top of the deck (again, supposedly a ten) and push it into the center of the deck.

5. A third time, pick up the card on top of the deck (again, supposedly a ten) and push it into the upper half of the deck, saying the third ghost entered the house by the back door.

6. Tell your audience that the fourth ghost stayed on the roof of the house to act as a lookout. Pick up the top card (a ten) and show it. Place it back on top of the deck.

7. Explain that you—the magician—were wandering around on Halloween night. Tell the audience that when you passed the house you scared all of the ghosts so badly that they all fled to the roof of the house.

8. Deal the four tens one at a time from the top of the deck, so everyone can see that the four tens (ghosts) have indeed magically appeared on the top of the deck (house).

JACK-O'-LANTERN THROUGH

HOW IT LOOKS

This is a trick that begins as a gag and ends as an illusion. You succeed in literally pushing a quarter-sized jack-o'-lantern through a hole the size of a dime in a piece of paper.

HOW TO MAKE IT

1. For this trick, you will need a piece of paper about the size of a dollar bill. Cut a hole exactly the size of a dime in the middle of the paper (**Figure 1**).

2. To make the jack-o'-lantern, glue small circles of orange construction paper to both sides of a quarter with water-soluble glue. Draw a face on one side with a felt-tip pen (**Figure 2**).

3. You will also need a pencil.

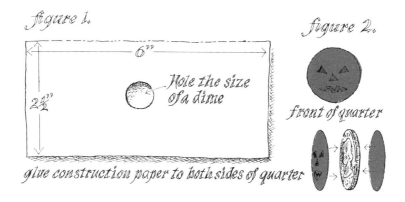

figure 1.

6"

2½"

Hole the size of a dime

figure 2.

front of quarter

glue construction paper to both sides of quarter

1. First, tell your friends that, because you are a magician, you can push the quarter-sized jack-o'-lantern through the smaller dime-sized hole in the piece of paper.

2. Lay the jack-o'-lantern on the table, hold the paper just above it, put the end of the pencil through the hole, and push the jack-o'-lantern with the pencil (**Figure 3**). You are pushing the jack-o'-lantern *through* the hole. No one will be impressed with this gag.

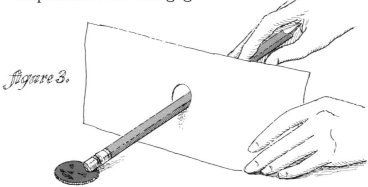

figure 3.

Now that your friends think they know the answer, you proceed to *really* push the jack-o'-lantern through the small hole. You will surprise yourself the first time you try this.

3. Lay the jack-o'-lantern on the paper so its edge is halfway over the hole (**Figure 4**).

4. Crease the paper in the center. Press the center down and pull the ends upward (**Figure 5**).

5. The little round hole will elongate into an oval and the jack-o'-lantern will drop through the hole and onto the table. The hole stays exactly the same size it was before.

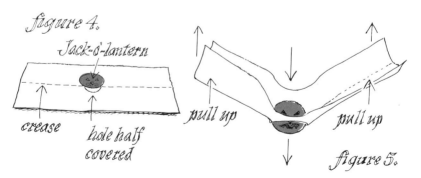

figure 4.

Jack-o'-lantern

crease

hole half covered

pull up

pull up

figure 5.

THE GHOST SOLVES A MYSTERY

HOW IT LOOKS

You hand a mystery book to a friend and show him a little paper ghost with a balloon coming from its mouth like the characters in comic strips. Have your friend look through the book and select a certain page, a certain line on that page, and a certain word in that line. Then have him do some math problems. You write something in the ghost's balloon. It is the word your friend selected. The ghost has solved the mystery.

HOW TO MAKE IT

For this trick, you will need a pencil, a piece of paper, and a mystery book. You will also need to draw a ghost on a piece of paper.

16

HOW TO DO IT

1. First, show the book and the paper ghost to the audience.

2. While you are not looking, have your friend choose any page above 99 in the book and write down the page number. Next, have him choose any line among the first 9 lines on that page and write down the number of the line. Then have him choose a word in that line among the first 9 words, counting left to right, and write down the number of the word and the word itself.

3. Have your friend multiply the page number by 2, multiply the result by 5, and add 20. Add the sum to the line number. Take that sum and add 5, multiply the result by 10, and add the number of the word on the line.

4. When your friend has finished his math, ask for his final answer.

5. You then page through the mystery book and write something in the ghost's balloon. It is the word your friend selected.

6. To find that word, you take your friend's result (a five-digit number) and subtract 250. The first three digits of your five-digit number tell you the page of the word your friend selected, the next digit tells you what line that word is on, and the last digit tells you the place of the word on the line. You simply find the word at that place in the book and write it in the ghost's balloon.

For example, if your friend selected the 7th word on line 4, page 122, his math would be like this:

The word he chose is on page 122   122
                                              $\times$ 2
                                                     244
                                              $\times$ 5
                                                    1220
                                              $+$ 20
                                                    1240
The word is on line 4 . . . . $+$ 4
                                                    1244
                                              $+$ 5
                                                    1249
                                              $\times$ 10
                                                   12490
The word is 7th on the line . . . . $+$ 7
To get his final answer   12497

You take his final answer	. . . .	12497
And subtract 250	. . . .	− 250
To get your result	. . . .	12247

You separate 12247 like this: 122-4-7. The word he chose is on page 122, the 4th line, and the 7th word on the line.

A HALLOWEEN PREDICTION

HOW IT LOOKS

You place three index cards on the table. One has a picture of a witch on it, one has a ghost, and one has a jack-o'-lantern. A volunteer from the audience chooses any one of the three cards. You predicted ahead of time which one would be chosen.

1. For this trick, you will need three index cards. Draw one picture—a witch, a ghost, and a jack-o'-lantern—on each card (**Figure 1**).

2. On the back of the ghost card, lightly write, "You will choose the ghost."

3. On a small slip of paper, write, "You will choose the witch." Place this slip of paper, along with the index cards, inside an envelope.

figure 1.

4. Make a magic wand by wrapping a piece of construction paper around a pencil, taping the paper, and removing the pencil (**Figure 2**). On a very small piece of paper, write, "You will choose the jack-o'-lantern." Roll up the paper and push it inside the magic wand.

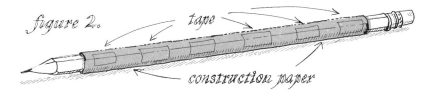

figure 2.   tape   construction paper

1. Take the witch, ghost, and jack-o'-lantern cards out of the envelope, making certain the pictures are face up, and lay the three cards side by side on the table. Be sure not to show the backs of the three cards and be sure to leave the slip of paper saying "You will choose the witch" hidden inside the envelope.

2. Point to the three cards with your magic wand. Ask a volunteer to choose one of the cards and tell everyone in the room which card she chose.

In this trick there are three *outs*. You will use a different *out* depending on which card the volunteer chooses.

3. a. If she chooses the ghost, tell her to turn over the three cards. You have correctly predicted the ghost.

b. If she selects the witch, leave the three cards face up on the table and hand her the envelope. Ask her to remove the slip of paper on which you have written your prediction. You have correctly predicted the witch.

c. If she chooses the jack-o'-lantern, leave the slip of paper inside the envelope, and use a pencil to push out the wad of paper hidden inside the wand. Hand the paper to the volunteer to read. You have correctly predicted the jack-o'-lantern.

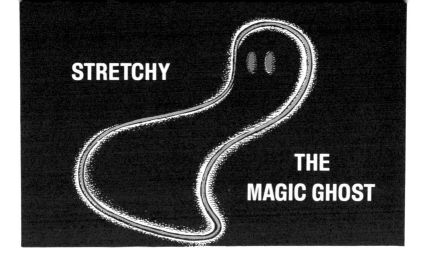

STRETCHY

THE
MAGIC GHOST

HOW IT LOOKS

Show a rubber band to the audience, which you introduce as Stretchy, the Magic Ghost. Hand Stretchy to a volunteer from the audience. Then have the volunteer tie a string around both of your wrists, leaving a length of string in between. The volunteer hands Stretchy back to you, you turn your back to the audience, and then turn again to face the audience. Stretchy is magically encircling the string, which is still tied to your wrists.

1. For this trick, you will need a piece of string about three feet (90 cm) long and two rubber bands which are exactly alike and which are big enough to slip easily over your fist. You will also need to be wearing a long-sleeved sweater.

2. Before you perform this trick, put one of the rubber bands around your wrist, pushed up under your sleeve (**Figure 1**). The audience does not know that this rubber band is there.

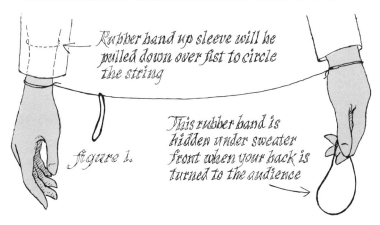

Rubber band up sleeve will be pulled down over fist to circle the string

figure 1.

This rubber band is hidden under sweater front when your back is turned to the audience

1. After introducing Stretchy (the rubber band that is *not* up your sleeve) to the audience, have a volunteer tie one end of the string to your left wrist and the other end to your right wrist. This will leave about two feet (60 cm) of string between your wrists. Take back the rubber band and turn your back to the audience.

2. As soon as your back is turned, stuff the original Stretchy under your sweater front and slip the rubber band that is up your sleeve over your fist and onto the string. Do this quickly. Then turn to face the audience, showing the rubber band magically encircling the string.

3. Tell the audience that Stretchy is a special ghost that not only can stretch, but can magically link itself onto a string tied between your wrists.

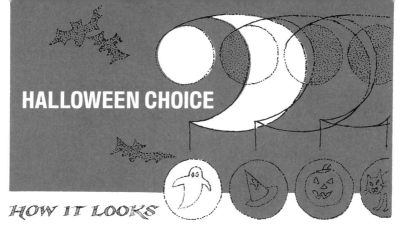

HALLOWEEN CHOICE

HOW IT LOOKS

Lying on a table are pictures of a broom, a black cat, a ghost, a jack-o'-lantern, and a witch's hat. In another room is your assistant. A volunteer from the audience chooses one of the five pictures as everyone else watches. Then he takes a pencil and a pad of paper to your assistant in the other room. She writes something on a sheet of paper and gives it to the volunteer. When you hold up the paper, everyone sees that your assistant has correctly named the picture selected. She can do this time and time again, naming the correct picture every time.

HOW TO MAKE IT

1. For this trick, you will need to draw pictures of a broom, a black cat, a ghost, a jack-o'-lantern, and a witch's hat on small individual pieces of paper (**Figure 1**).

figure 1.

2. You will also need four pencils that are the same color and look the same, but are slightly different in length. You and your assistant will have to memorize that the shortest pencil stands for a broom, the next size stands for a black cat, the next for a ghost, and the longest for a jack-o'-lantern. (That is easy to do because the objects are in alphabetical order: *B*room, *C*at, *G*host, *J*ack-o'-lantern, that is B, C, G, and J.)

3. You will also need a pad of paper with the length of the four pencils marked on the back of the pad with light dots (**Figure 2**).

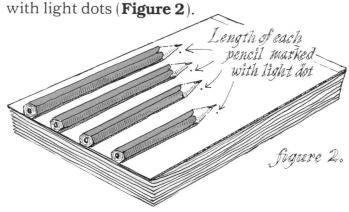

Length of each pencil marked with light dot

figure 2.

1. The pad of paper is on the table face-up but the four pencils are kept in different pockets out of sight from the audience. Remember which pocket contains which size pencil.

2. Once the volunteer selects the picture, you signal that information to your assistant by which pencil you send her with the pad.

3. When your assistant gets the pad and pencil, she measures the pencil she receives along the back of the pad. In this way, she determines which of the pictures was selected: the shortest pencil means the broom; the next size means the black cat; the next size means the ghost; the longest means the jack-o'-lantern.

4. If the witch's hat is selected, you simply borrow a pencil from someone in the audience. When your assistant receives a strange pencil along with the pad, she will automatically know the witch's hat has been chosen.

GHOST ON THE WALL

HOW IT LOOKS

You ask a friend if she believes you can make her see a Halloween ghost. When she says no, you prove you can do it.

HOW TO MAKE IT

For this trick, you will need the drawing in **Figure 1**.

1. Tell your friend to look steadily at **Figure 1** under a strong light. She must keep her eyes on the tiny cross in the picture for about 60 seconds.

2. Then have her look at a white wall or a white sheet of paper. As she looks, a large ghostly image of the picture will appear before her eyes. She will be surprised at how clear the image is. It can be made clearer by blinking a few times.

This is an example of how you can convert an optical illusion into a magic trick.

figure 1.

IN THE TRICK-OR-TREAT BAG

HOW IT LOOKS

You tell the audience that there are some candies in a small trick-or-treat bag, but you don't tell them how many. Then you have a volunteer do some math. His final answer is the exact number of candies in the bag—even though this does not seem possible.

34

figure 1.

HOW TO MAKE IT

1. For this trick, you will need three flat hard candies or mints. Break one candy in half (**Figure 1**). (You will only use one half of the candy.)

2. Decorate a small paper bag to look like a trick-or-treat bag.

3. Put the two whole candies and the half candy in your pocket and the trick-or-treat bag on a table.

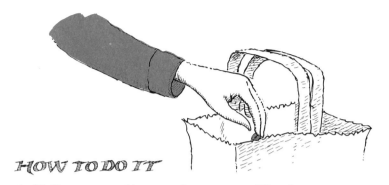

1. Tell your audience that you will take some candies out of your pocket and put them in the trick-or-treat bag, but that you will not tell them how many. Then take out the 2½ candies and put them into the bag without letting anyone see them. Set the bag aside and tell the audience they will see exactly how many candies are in the bag later.

2. Choose a volunteer and tell him to choose any number, add it to the next highest number, add 9, divide by 2, subtract the original number, and divide by 2 again, without letting you see what he writes.

For example:

The number he chose 23

Plus the next highest number . . . . $\underline{+\ 24}$

47

Plus 9 . . . . $\underline{+\ 9}$

Divided by 2 . . . . $56 \div 2 = 28$

Minus the original number . . . . $\underline{-\ 23}$

Divided by 2 to get his final answer . . . . $5 \div 2\ =\ 2\frac{1}{2}$

3. Tell the volunteer his final answer is the *exact* number of candies you put in the trick-or-treat bag at the beginning. The volunteer will think you made a mistake because his final answer is $2\frac{1}{2}$ and you would not put $2\frac{1}{2}$ candies in the trick-or-treat bag.

4. You ask him for his final answer.

5. When he says "$2\frac{1}{2}$," you should look puzzled as if you don't know what went "wrong." Then you smile and say, "I guess I'll have to treat you to a trick." Empty the trick-or-treat bag onto the table. Out roll exactly $2\frac{1}{2}$ candies.

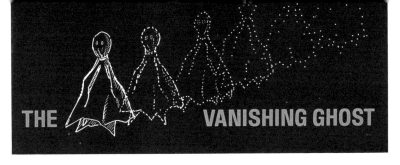

THE VANISHING GHOST

Show a ghost, made from a marble and a piece of white cloth, to an audience of at least five people. You hold the ghost in one hand and cover it with a handkerchief. Let three or four members of the audience reach under the handkerchief to make sure the ghost is there. Suddenly, you pull the handkerchief away and the ghost has vanished even though members of the audience felt it under the handkerchief. Next, you cover your empty hand with the handkerchief and let members of the audience reach under the handkerchief again to make sure your hand is empty. After several people do this, you whisk away the handkerchief — and the ghost has magically reappeared.

For this trick, you will need a handkerchief and the ghost. To make the ghost, cover a large marble with a small piece of white cloth and tie the cloth in place with white thread (**Figure 1**). Draw a face on the ghost with a felt-tip pen.

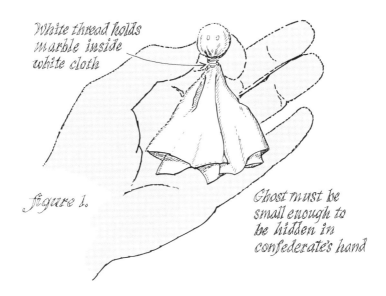

White thread holds marble inside white cloth

figure 1.

Ghost must be small enough to be hidden in confederate's hand

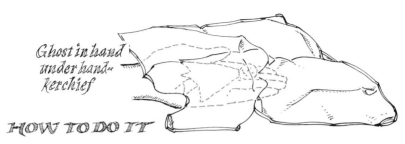

Ghost in hand under handkerchief

HOW TO DO IT

For this baffling trick, you will need a *confederate*, or a person who, unknown to the audience, helps you with the trick. (As a magician, the occasional use of a confederate is all right, but you should not over-use this method.)

1. Ask a few random people to reach under the handkerchief. They all agree the ghost is there because they can feel the ghost.

2. Lastly, ask your confederate to reach under. He says "Yes, the ghost is still there" but at the same time he hides the ghost in his hand and brings it out, unknown to the others.

3. You then pull away the handkerchief, showing the ghost has disappeared.

4. The ghost reappears the same way. The confederate is the last person you ask to reach under the handkerchief. When he does, the confederate puts the ghost back on your hand under the handkerchief.

This is an excellent stunt to pull at a Halloween party when a lot of people are around.

COLOR-CHANGING JACK-O'-LANTERNS

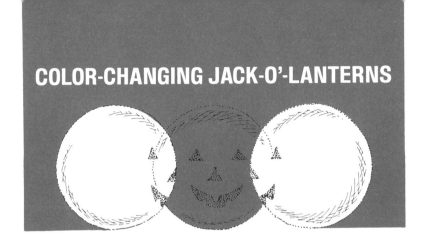

HOW IT LOOKS

A small orange jack-o'-lantern is wrapped in an orange handkerchief or scarf and lowered into a glass. A small white jack-o'-lantern is wrapped in a white handkerchief and lowered into a second glass across the room (Figure 1). The magician says a magic word—"Halloween"—and lifts the orange handkerchief to reveal the white jack-o'-lantern. He lifts the white handkerchief to reveal the orange jack-o'-lantern. The two have magically changed place.

figure 1.

Two white jack-o'-lanterns, figure 2.

One orange jack-o'-lantern

HOW TO MAKE IT

For this trick, you will need two white Ping-Pong balls and one orange Ping-Pong ball to make three jack-o'-lanterns (**Figure 2**). Draw the eyes, nose and mouth on all three Ping-Pong balls with a black felt-tip pen. You will also need two hand-kerchiefs or scarves, one white and one orange.

HOW TO DO IT

When you begin the trick there should be two glasses, one white and one orange scarf, and one white and one orange jack-o'-lantern on the table. The other white jack-o'-lantern is in your hand, but the audience does not realize this. They think that only two jack-o'-lanterns are used.

1. You pick up the orange jack-o'-lantern and place it under the orange scarf.

2. Unknown to the audience, you have had the other white jack-o'-lantern in your hand from the beginning. Once your hand is under the scarf, substitute the white jack-o'-lantern for the orange jack-o'-lantern.

3. Lower the orange scarf, now containing the white jack-o'-lantern, into the glass.

4. Bring out your hand with the orange jack-o'-lantern hidden in your palm. (Don't look at your hand, and the audience won't look either.)

5. Pick up the white jack-o'-lantern from the table and place it under the white scarf.

6. When your hand is under the scarf, substitute the orange jack-o'-lantern for the white one. Wrap the orange jack-o'-lantern in the scarf, and push it into the glass.

7. Step back, wave your left hand—the one not holding the third jack-o'-lantern—and say the magic word, "Halloween." While doing so, simply slip the third jack-o'-lantern—the one in your right hand—into your pocket.

8. Walk over to the first glass. Slowly pull out the orange scarf and reveal the white jack-o'-lantern. Then pull out the white scarf and reveal the orange jack-o'-lantern. The two jack-o'-lanterns have magically changed places.

TRICKS FOR BETTER MAGIC

Here are some simple rules you should keep in mind while learning to perform the tricks in this book.

1. Read the entire trick several times until you thoroughly understand it.
2. Practice the trick alone or in front of a mirror until you feel comfortable doing the trick, then present it to an audience.
3. Learn to perform one trick perfectly before moving on to another trick. It is better to perform one trick well than a half dozen poorly.
4. Work on your "presentation." Make up special "patter" (what you say while doing a trick) that is funny and entertaining. Even the simplest trick becomes magical when it is properly presented.
5. Choose tricks that suit you and your personality. Some tricks will work better for you than others.

Stick with these. *Every* trick is not meant to be performed by *every* magician.

6. Feel free to experiment and change a trick to suit you and your unique personality so that you are more comfortable presenting it.

7. Never reveal the secret of the trick. Your audience will respect you much more if you do not explain the trick. When asked how you did a trick, simply say "by magic."

8. Never repeat a trick for the same audience. If you do, you will have lost the element of surprise and your audience will probably figure out how you did it the second time around.

9. Take your magic seriously, but not yourself. Have fun with magic and your audience will have fun along with you.

ABOUT THE AUTHOR

James W. Baker, a magician for over 30 years, has performed as "Mister Mystic" in hospitals, orphanages, and schools around the world. He is a member of the International Brotherhood of Magicians and the Society of American Magicians, and is author of *Illusions Illustrated*, a magic book for young performers.

From 1951 to 1963, Baker was a reporter for *The Richmond (VA) News Leader*. From 1963 to 1983, he was an editor with the U.S. Information Agency, living in Washington, D.C., India, Turkey, Pakistan, the Philippines, and Tunisia, and traveling in 50 other countries. Today Baker and his wife, Elaine, live in Williamsburg, Virginia, where he performs magic and writes for the local newspaper, *The Virginia Gazette*.

ABOUT THE ARTIST

George Overlie is a talented artist who has illustrated numerous books. Born in the small town of Rose Creek, Minnesota, Overlie graduated from the New York Phoenix School of Design and began his career as a layout artist. He soon turned to book illustration and proved his skill and versatility in this demanding field. For Overlie, fantasy, illusion, and magic are all facets of illustration and have made doing the Holiday Magic books a real delight.